The earliest dinosaurs were little meat-eaters, like *Chindesaurus* (CHIN-dee-saw-rus). It lived in the Late Triassic Period. *Chindesaurus* had to be careful. Giant meat-eaters like *Smilosuchus* (SMY-luh-SOOK-us), a relative of crocodiles, liked to eat these small early dinosaurs.

Smilosuchus lived in lakes and rivers. Another giant crocodile relative, *Poposaurus* (POH-poh-saw-rus), chased *Chindesaurus* on land. But the early dinosaurs survived! And some grew bigger and BIGGER!

DINOSAURS!

Dinosaurs ruled the world for 160 million years. Some had fins. Some had big horns. Some had armor like a tank. The biggest were ten times larger than an elephant!

We find out about dinosaurs by digging up *fossils*—bones and footprints buried in sand and mud that've turned into rock. That's what I do. I'm a paleontologist (pay-lee-uhn-TAH-luh-jist).

Dinosaurs didn't all live at the same time. There were three dinosaur periods—the Triassic (try-ASS-ick), the Jurassic (juh-RASS-ick), and the Cretaceous (krih-TAY-shus). At the end of each period, many kinds of animals died out—they became *extinct*.

The three periods together make up the Mesozoic (meh-zuh-ZOH-ick) Era. Almost all the dinosaurs died out at the end of the Mesozoic, 65 million years ago.

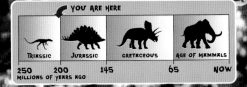

Many dinosaurs became huge—bigger than elephants—in the Jurassic Period! *Stegosaurus* (STEG-uh-saw-rus) lived in the Late Jurassic. It was a plant-eater with armor plates sticking out of its back and sharp spikes on its tail.

YOU ARE HERE

| TRIASSIC | JURASSIC | CRETACEOUS | AGE OF MAMMALS |

250 200   145   65   NOW
MILLIONS OF YEARS AGO

Stegosaurus fought a big Jurassic meat-eater called *Allosaurus* (AL-uh-saw-rus). We dug up an *Allosaurus* skeleton that had a hole in its hipbone. The hole fit the tail spike of a stegosaur. So we know the stegosaur had scored a direct hit.

Many giant long-necked dinosaurs lived in the Late Jurassic Period.
We dug up the footprints of a baby *Apatosaurus* (uh-PAT-uh-saw-rus).
Danger was nearby! Close to the baby's tracks we found tracks from a
huge meat-eater, *Torvosaurus* (TOR-vuh-saw-rus).

YOU ARE HERE

TRIASSIC	JURASSIC	CRETACEOUS	AGE OF MAMMALS

250   200   145   65   NOW
MILLIONS OF YEARS AGO

But the baby *Apatosaurus* was safe. Right next to its tracks were the footprints of an adult *Apatosaurus,* probably its mother or father. An adult *Apatosaurus* fought with its long, whiplike tail. The tail was 30 feet long—as long as a school bus!

Fossil teeth tell us that meat-eaters worked hard to raise their babies. Dinosaurs lost teeth when they fed. And then they grew new ones. They grew new teeth all through their lives. Crocodiles do that today.

We dug up the bones of a *Brachiosaurus* (BRACK-ee-uh-saw-rus), a Late Jurassic plant-eater. And mixed in with the bones, we found teeth from an adult and a baby *Ceratosaurus* (suh-RAT-uh-saw-rus)— a meat-eater. That means the ceratosaur adult and baby ate together— just like a mom lion does with her cubs.

During the Cretaceous Period,
some dinosaurs became very fast and
very smart. *Deinonychus* (dy-NON-ih-kus)
was a meat-eater that lived in the Early
Cretaceous. It was only as heavy as a big dog.

But *Deinonychus* was speedy and had a big brain. Packs of *Deinonychus* attacked like kickboxers. They slashed with their super-sharp hind claws. That's why *Deinonychus* could kill large plant-eaters like the long-tailed *Tenontosaurus* (teh-NON-tuh-saw-rus).

The Late Cretaceous dinosaurs grew the biggest fins and frills. *Spinosaurus* (SPY-nuh-saw-rus) was a gigantic fish-eater with a sail on its back. The sail made its body look taller and scarier.

Spinosaurs fought each other over the best fishing spots. They would huff and puff and stand on their tiptoes trying to frighten each other. Lizards with tall sails fight this way today.

YOU ARE HERE

| TRIASSIC | JURASSIC | CRETACEOUS | AGE OF MAMMALS |

| 250 | 200 | 145 | 65 | NOW |
MILLIONS OF YEARS AGO

YOU ARE HERE

| TRIASSIC | JURASSIC | CRETACEOUS | AGE OF MAMMALS |

250   200   145   65   NOW
MILLIONS OF YEARS AGO

Parasaurolophus (PAR-uh-sawr-OH-loaf-us) was a Late Cretaceous plant-eater. Its nickname is "Trombone Dinosaur." It had a head with a crest of bone that stuck out behind. Inside the crest was a tube. When a *Parasaurolophus* snorted, its breath went up through the tube. The noise was so loud and so low, it made the ground shake!

Parasaurolophus herds used the noise to call to each other miles away. *Hypacrosaurus* (hy-PACK-ruh-saw-rus) was a close relative that had a curved crest on its head for noisemaking.

Torosaurus (TOR-uh-saw-rus) was a plant-eater with long horns. It lived 66 million years ago, at the very end of the Mesozoic Era. *Torosaurus* had the biggest, strongest head of any dinosaur. Its skull was eight feet long!

Torosaurus needed its long horns and strong head to fight the meat-eater *Tyrannosaurus* (ty-RAN-uh-saw-rus). *Tyrannosaurus* had the strongest jaws and thickest teeth of any meat-eating dinosaur. One bite could crush a hipbone or rib cage.

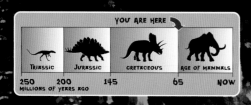

YOU ARE HERE

TRIASSIC | JURASSIC | CRETACEOUS | AGE OF MAMMALS
250   200   145   65   NOW
MILLIONS OF YEARS AGO

Plant-eaters fought each other, too. Male plant-eaters would fight to impress females. *Stygimoloch* (STIJ-ih-MOH-lock) was a plant-eater the size of a sheep. It had a built-in helmet made from bone and a thick neck like a football player. One *Stygimoloch* would try to ram another *Stygimoloch* in the stomach.

Edmontonia (ED-mun-TONE-ee-yuh) was an armored plant-eater with spikes on its shoulders. The spikes were long and sharp. One blow could kill a *Tyrannosaurus*.

Microraptor (MY-kroh-RAP-tur) was a tiny relative of *Deinonychus*. It lived in the Early Cretaceous and was no larger than a big crow. *Microraptor* had long fingers with sharp claws. It could climb trees by digging its claws into the bark.

And *Microraptor* could soar like a flying squirrel! Fossils dug in China show that *Microraptor* skin was covered in feathers, just like a bird's!

That means . . .

. . . some dinosaurs are still alive today. All birds—ostriches and hummingbirds, eagles and parrots—came from an ancestor like *Microraptor*. When you pet a parakeet, you're petting a genuine great-great-GREAT-grandchild of a dinosaur!

Dino Babies!

Were dinosaurs good parents?

If you were a baby *T. rex*, would your mom or dad be there to protect you? Or would you be left on your own?

What if you were a *Triceratops* (try-SEHR-uh-tops) kid, and a big meat-eater tried to grab you? Would your mom or dad rush in to save you?

There are many kinds of animal parents. A turtle mom lays her eggs in a nest, covers them with sand, then walks away. She never sees her babies again.

A crocodile mom stays close to her nest. She chases away lizards who try to steal the eggs. She protects the newly hatched crocs for up to a year.

Eagle and hawk parents work even harder. They feed their young until they're fully grown.

Were dino moms and dads like turtles? Or crocodiles?
Or eagles? Or something in between?

    I'm a paleontologist (pay-lee-uhn-TAH-luh-jist),
a scientist who studies fossils. Paleontologists study
dino families by digging up bones, teeth, eggs,
and footprints left behind in rock layers.

Fossil teeth can tell us how dino babies got their food. When dinos ate, some of their teeth would fall out, and new teeth would grow in. I found a spot in Wyoming full of baby teeth from *Allosaurus* (AL-uh-saw-rus), a meat-eater.

The babies had been eating huge chunks of plant-eating dinosaurs. How did the babies get such big hunks of meat?

From their parents! We found giant teeth from adult *Allosaurus* mixed with the baby teeth. *Allosaurus* moms and dads brought food to their young. The babies didn't have to hunt by themselves.

Today, many birds make rookeries—spots where hundreds of nests are crowded together. Did dinosaurs use rookeries?

Some did! In Argentina, we found thousands of dino eggs in hundreds of nests, all buried in mud that had turned into stone.

All the eggs came from titanosaurs (ty-TAN-oh-sawrs), long-necked plant-eaters bigger than elephants.

Dozens of the eggs had the bones of unhatched babies inside. They were no bigger than kittens.

The nests were so close together that the moms and dads had to walk very carefully so that they didn't step on the eggs. Or the babies!

Did long-necked dinosaurs take care of their kids after they left the nest?
Yes! Here's how we know:

In Texas, we dug up huge fossil footprints from long-necked brachiosaurs (BRACK-ee-uh-sawrs). They were walking in a big herd. And there were small tracks too, made by youngsters hurrying to keep up with the adults.

The adult brachiosaurs were strong enough to easily crunch any predator who tried to grab a brachiosaur kid.

Not all dino moms and dads were big. Adult *Drinker*s were plant-eating dinos about the size of turkeys. I found a dozen *Drinker* skeletons, babies and adults, all crowded together in one spot in Wyoming.

What were the *Drinker*s doing there?

We x-rayed the rock. The X-ray showed that all the dinosaurs were sitting down side by side, feet flat on the ground, and facing the same direction.

It was an entire dino family in their burrow! Animals use burrows as shelters from bad weather, and to hide from predators in.

Today, ostrich dads are great babysitters. They'll guard up to forty chicks at once!

Psittacosaurus (sih-TAK-oh-saw-rus) was a dinosaur babysitter. The adult was the size of a big chicken. Three dozen baby *Psittacosaurus* were found in Mongolia, all crowded around just one adult. Maybe it was Mom. Maybe it was Dad. Either way, he or she had a tough job!

Psittacosaurus ate leaves, roots, and bugs. And lots of plants and bugs are poisonous. The babies probably watched what Mom or Dad ate. That way, they learned what to eat and what to avoid.

Many plant-eating dino moms could call to their babies by blowing through tubes in their snouts. *Parasaurolophus* (PAR-uh-sawr-OH-loaf-us), found in New Mexico, had really long sound tubes.

Babies didn't have big tubes, so they just went *squeak*. But Mom could *HONK* so loud she could make the ground shake.

Moms could call to their kids from far away. *"Hey! Come back here!"* is what the call meant.

When a meat-eater attacked, a dozen *Parasaurolophus* moms might all honk at once—and give the meat-eater a splitting headache!

Adult *Triceratops* were big and dangerous. They used their long, sharp horns and massive muscles to fight *T. rex*.

But baby *Triceratops* were only as big as sheep, and their horns were slender and weak. Did their parents protect them?

Yes! Baby T'tops teeth are always found with adult T'tops teeth. If the babies were ever by themselves, we'd find just baby teeth.

A *T. rex* who tried to snatch a *Triceratops* baby might be charged by an angry mom or dad—or both! That would have been scary!

Imagine that you are a *T. rex* baby in your nest on a dark, chilly night. What would you feel? Your mom's warm body!

T. rex wasn't a big lizard with naked, scaly skin. Fossil skin found on tyrannosaur skeletons shows thin, hairlike feathers. That proves that rexes were hot-blooded—they had enough body heat to keep themselves and their babies warm even when it was cold outside.

Who were the very *best* dino moms and dads?
That's a tough question, but I vote for raptors!
Deinonychus (dy-NON-ih-kus) was a fast, graceful raptor the size of a wolf.
A *Deinonychus* skeleton found in Montana showed that when the dino died, it had
been sitting on its eggs. The raptor was using its arms and body to protect its

unhatched babies. Those arms had big, strong feathers! We've found many raptor skeletons preserved with skin, and all show a complete set of wide feathers, similar to a hawk's or eagle's.

Raptors had big brains. This means raptor parents were intelligent—they could play with their chicks and teach them how to hunt and outsmart enemies.

Wouldn't it be wonderful to see a live raptor? Well, we can! Modern-day birds are descendants of raptors. When you watch a mom or dad eagle feeding its babies, you are seeing a living *Deinonychus*!

PREHISTORIC MONSTERS!

I'm a paleontologist (pay-lee-uhn-TAH-luh-jist). I hunt fossils—buried remains of animals that lived long ago. Fossils tell us how the first life-forms changed into weird and spectacular creatures.

Prehistoric time is divided into "eras." The first era was the Precambrian. It started over 3 billion years ago. There weren't any animals at all during most of the Precambrian. And the only fossils come from simple seaweeds called algae.

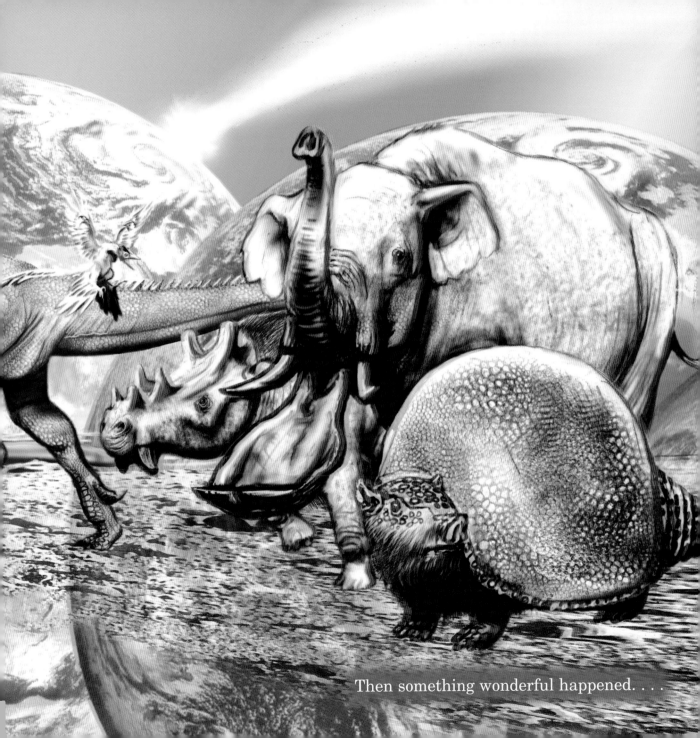

Then something wonderful happened. . . .

trilobites

The Paleozoic (pay-lee-uh-ZOH-ick) Era began about 540 million years ago. Suddenly the oceans were full of creatures with shells. The most common shelled critters had long feelers and bodies divided into three sections— trilobites (TRY-luh-bites)! The name means "three-sectioned animals."

Trilobites scurried around the sea bottom on little crab-like feet. They also swam and dug in the sand and mud.

nautiloid

YOU ARE HERE

Precambrian Paleozoic Mesozoic Cenozoic
600   500   400   300   200   100   Now
millions of years ago

Trilobite shells were suits of armor put together with hinges. Most trilobites could curl up into a ball, the way some armadillos can. And many grew horns and spikes. Why? Because trilobites had enemies—the nautiloids—who had tentacles for grabbing and jaws for crunching trilobite victims!

Pteraspis

In the Middle
Paleozoic—about
400 million years ago—
a new kind of monster predator
appeared . . . sea scorpions! They
looked like today's land scorpions but
lived in salt water and grew to twelve feet long.

sea scorpion

Sea scorpions didn't have stingers. Instead, they grabbed their victims with spiked pincers and chewed them up with strong jaws that worked sideways. Many fish had to grow thick armor to protect themselves.

The earliest fish were only a foot or two long. But then—about 380 million years ago—super-sized armored fish as big as killer whales appeared! *Gorgonichthys* (gore-gun-ICK-theez) was one of the snap-headed sharks. They attacked with big fangs up front and slicing teeth in the back. Their teeth were self-sharpening and were like a pair of strong scissors.

Dinichthys

spiny shark

Gorgonichthys

Gorgonichthys had a special joint that let its entire head snap down with startling speed and force. *Gorgonichthys* would open its mouth really wide, then . . . *kee-RUNCH!*

Meanwhile, another kind of fish was doing something incredible! Over millions of years, the four fins of these fish changed into four legs, with toes for walking on land. These four-legged fish became amphibians, laying their eggs in water, frog-style. *Anthracosaurus* (an-THRACK-uh-sore-us) was an early amphibian as big as a crocodile—and just as fierce.

Amphibians couldn't go very far onto land because they needed water to breed. But then one type of amphibian changed in a very special way. It laid eggs on land, like a turtle, and became the first reptile. Now the reptiles could spread all over dry land. *Dimetrodon* (dy-MEH-truh-dahn) was a reptile that grew as big as a lion. It hunted plant-eating reptiles and big amphibians and swamp sharks with poison spines on their heads.

Dimetrodon and its kin had tall fins on their backs. The fins made the creatures look scarier. My crew is digging up *Dimetrodon* fossils right now in the red rocks of North Texas.

Anthracosaurus

YOU ARE HERE

Precambrian | Paleozoic | Mesozoic | Cenozoic

600 500 400 300 200 100 Now
millions of years ago

Dimetrodon

Edaphosaurus

When the Paleozoic Era ended—250 million years ago—the Mesozoic (meh-zuh-ZOH-ick) Era began. Reptiles kept on changing and changing. . . .

Some reptiles evolved into sea monsters. Giant four-flippered pliosaurs (PLY-uh-sorz) had heads ten feet long. Ichthyosaurs (ICK-thee-uh-sorz), or fish-lizards, developed bodies shaped like fast-swimming sharks.

In the Late Mesozoic, new sea reptiles appeared. Sea turtles grew to be ten feet wide. The most graceful swimming reptiles were the swan lizards, or elasmosaurs (ih-LAS-muh-sorz). They used their long necks to snag prey underwater.

ichthyosaurs

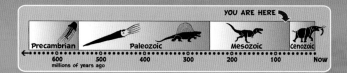

YOU ARE HERE

Precambrian Paleozoic Mesozoic Cenozoic

600   500   400   300   200   100   Now
millions of years ago

sea turtle

pliosaur

elasmosaur

Meanwhile, on land, another Mesozoic reptile group evolved into the most famous prehistoric monsters of all—the dinosaurs! The mighty *Tyrannosaurus rex* ran on long, strong hind legs like a giant turkey.

Many meat-eating dinos had feathers! In fact, tiny meat-eating dinosaurs evolved into birds. There were other Mesozoic fliers, too—giant pterodactyls (tehr-uh-DACK-tulz). *Quetzalcoatlus* (kwet-sul-kuh-WHAT-lus) could zoom down and scare a *T. rex*.

Anatosaurus

Tyrannosaurus rex

YOU ARE HERE

Precambrian   Paleozoic   Mesozoic   Cenozoic

600   500   400   300   200   100   Now
millions of years ago

Quetzalcoatlus

baby *T. rex*

About 65 million years ago, the Mesozoic Era ended and the Cenozoic (seh-nuh-ZOH-ick) Era began. All the dinosaurs died out. But their little relatives, the birds, kept going.

The new rulers of the land were mammals—creatures with hair and fur. *Eobasileus* (ee-oh-buh-SILL-ee-us) was as big as an elephant and had saber teeth eight inches long, plus six horns for butting.

Eobasileus

But—surprise!—*Eobasileus* ate only plants!
Its saber teeth were for fighting other *Eobasileus*
and frightening meat-eaters.

waterbirds

Harpagolestes

YOU ARE HERE

Precambrian | Paleozoic | Mesozoic | Cenozoic

600 | 500 | 400 | 300 | 200 | 100 | Now
millions of years ago

In the Late Cenozoic Era—10 million years ago—there were lots of mastodons, or elephant relatives. *Platybelodon* (plaa-tee-BELL-uh-dahn) was a shovel-jawed mastodon. Its pointed upper tusks were good for fighting saber-toothed cats. The two lower tusks made a wide scoop just like a shovel!

Platybelodon

What did *Platybelodon* do with its shovel jaw?
We haven't solved that mystery yet. Maybe it
scooped up water lilies. Or dug sweet potatoes. Or
carried baby *Platybelodon* when it got tired.

I helped dig up some shovel-tuskers in Mongolia.
Their skulls were the weirdest I've ever seen!

saber-toothed cat

YOU ARE HERE

Precambrian   Paleozoic   Mesozoic   Cenozoic

600   500   400   300   200   100   Now
millions of years ago

woolly mammoths

Later in the Cenozoic Era—3 million years ago—ice layers a mile thick spread over the land. Mammals grew heavy fur coats to stay warm.

Some elephants grew shaggy hair and became woolly mammoths. And some rhinos grew shaggy coats and became woolly rhinoceroses. Some lions grew shaggy coats, too.

There was a new predator, the most dangerous animal of all time. It didn't have fangs or claws or horns. But it was dangerously smart! Who was it? Its scientific name is *Homo sapiens* (HO-mo SAY-pee-unz).

woolly
rhinoceros

YOU ARE HERE

Precambrian | Paleozoic | Mesozoic | Cenozoic
600 | 500 | 400 | 300 | 200 | 100 | Now
millions of years ago

Homo sapiens

It was us! Human beings! Ice Age humans
made elegant spears and stone knives. And they
hunted reindeer, wild horses, bears, and mammoths
and made warm clothes from their hides.

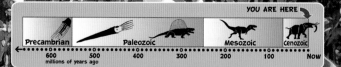

YOU ARE HERE

Precambrian · Paleozoic · Mesozoic · Cenozoic

600 · 500 · 400 · 300 · 200 · 100 · Now

millions of years ago

Homo sapiens

glyptodon

Humans spread from Africa to Europe and Asia, and then to America, where they hunted giant sloths and glyptodons (GLIP-tuh-dahnz)—armadillo-like mammals as big as hippos.

Ice Age humans painted beautiful pictures of horses and bulls and rhinos on cave walls, and they carved sculptures of shaggy mammoths and buffalo.

Homo sapiens

These people were our ancestors! Our great-great-*great* . . . grandmothers and grandfathers!

I'm proud to be a descendant of those hunter-artists. I hope you are, too!